NEWTON FERRERS & NOSS MAYO

Chips Barber

To Wembury Bay ←

River Yealm

Newton Ferrers

Holy Cross Church

Bridgend

The Creek

The Dolphin

Noss Mayo

St Peter's Church

The Swan Inn

The Old Ship Inn

Best wishes!
Chips Barber

OBELISK PUBLICATIONS

*We have over 140 Devon titles – for full list please send SAE to
Obelisk Publications, 2 Church Hill, Pinhoe, Exeter EX4 9ER
or telephone 01392 468556*

Plate Acknowledgements

Many thanks to Brian Carter for permission to use his sketch map from *Walks in the South Hams*, on title page. Thanks also to Jack Crocker for picture on page 23; John and Jenie Allen for pictures on pages 4, 9 (top), 12, 13, 22, 31 (middle); Michael Ashton for pictures on page 7 (top), 16, 17, 20, 25; Kath Powley for pages 5, 6, 9 (bottom), 28; Jane Reynolds for drawing of Membland Hall on page 21; and Jack Hockaday for pictures on pages 8, 24 and 32.

All other pictures by or belonging to Chips Barber.

*First published in 1996 by
Obelisk Publications, 2 Church Hill, Pinhoe, Exeter, Devon
Designed and Typeset by Sally Barber
Printed in Great Britain by
Devonshire Press Limited, Torquay, Devon*

© Chips Barber/Obelisk Publications 1996

NEWTON FERRERS & NOSS MAYO

The last time that I gave a talk to the Newton & Noss WI, in their cosy, compact hall at Newton Ferrers, I was quizzed, 'in the nicest possible way', as to why I had left Newton Ferrers and Noss Mayo out of the various books that I had written. Having now put the effort into producing this little book, I must admit that I, too, wonder why they have been neglected for so long!

It is true that my links with the place are somewhat tenuous, but they do go back a reasonably long time – initially to when I was a student and worked on traffic surveys, then later, once I had discovered the delights of these charming twin villages, I organised walks in the area with various rambling groups.

In more recent years I had the pleasant task of taking photographs for television presenter David Young's *A-Z of Villages* as he so wisely decided that 'N' should stand for these two villages.

Of course just visiting a place is not quite the same as having lived in it but this book has been put together with a lot of thought and effort. It was both a pleasure and a privilege to meet and talk with various villagers, to hear their stories, opinions and thoughts on a community that I had only seen before as an observer. Things certainly start to take on a new perspective when seen through other folks' eyes, that is the people who love their own villages!

Although this is not a history book it's important to consider where the 'Ferrers' came from in Newton's name. You have to go back the best part of a thousand years to the times when William, Duke of Normandy was planning to invade our shores. In the southern part of his native Normandy one of the richest men was Henry de Ferrers who owned the biggest iron mines in that part of the world. He pledged his support to William's cause, the reward being the receipt of some 200 manors in this country. Many were in Derbyshire but they were spread the length and breadth of the country. Other 'Ferrers' will also be found in Northants, Essex and Somerset. In Devon alone we also have Churston Ferrers and Bere Ferrers, that delightful spot where the tidal waters of the Tamar and Tavy merge. The Ferrers family derived their name from the French word for blacksmith, in fact their family coat of arms depicts three horse shoes. If you have a good map you may be able to locate Henry's home patch, which is called Ferrière St Hilaire, found in southern Normandy.

The Rev Hugh Grimes must have been something of a live-wire for his name kept popping up when I was putting this book together. When he was 89, in 1962, he proposed the idea that Newton Ferrers should preserve that historical link and twin with Ferrière St Hilaire.

In England there are 31 Newtons without any additional qualifying suffixes or prefixes and there are almost a hundred others (97 to be precise) like Newton Ferrers that have a further name to help qualify them, of which there are also several examples in Devon. These include Newton Abbot, Newton Petrock, Newton Tracey, Newton St Cyres and Newton Poppleford (which has a main street as long as its name!). But there is only one Noss!

The settlements of Newton and Noss have developed on an inlet that branches off the Yealm estuary. When the tide is in it looks like a major river valley only to end in an abrupt fashion, the maritime equivalent of a cul-de-sac.

For some strange reason it is true that these twin villages have had a raw deal from the writers of guide books, probably because they are only small places and not true tourist resorts in the accepted sense of the word. Those visitors it does get, however, initially are sure to pronounce Yealm as if it rhymes with realm, when all self-respecting and fully-initiated folk know it should rhyme with ram! To enforce this point a former owner of the River Yealm Hotel, James Ford, had a boat called the 'Yam Yam'. It was an ex-Admiralty steam pinnace, used to ferry guests to and from his hotel and Steer Point. This entrepreneur took full advantage of the newly-created branch line of the Great Western Railway, from Plymouth to Yealmpton.

This hotel, built about 1898, enjoys a superb position. An early guide book claimed that its site was the 'Beauty Spot of Devon'; for a mere three and a half to five guineas per week one could enjoy many luxuries, not least professional hairdressing and 'violet ray' treatment, on the premises!

There were several steamboats operating in the district. Bought by Captain Hodge, the *Puffing Billy* was the forerunner of the *Kitley Belle*, also operating a regular ferry service from Newton Creek to Steer Point.

The *Hibernia, Alexandra, Empress* and the *Princess Royal* were just some of the paddle steamers to make the journey from Plymouth, which, in reasonable weather, took

Princess Royal

about 45 minutes. There were times when competing firms showed their rivalry by sailing dangerously close to each other across Wembury Bay and up the Yealm when there were miles of open sea at their disposal. On Bank Holidays many hundreds of Plymothians would take the opportunity of enjoying a ferry ride to the Yealm. However, the advent of the motor car and charabanc, and the removal of tolls on the two bridges at Laira, both played their part in the decline in popularity of the sea voyage between Plymouth and the Yealm.

Likewise the fishing industry at Newton and Noss, once so important, as it was all along the South Devon coastline, has ground to an almost ignominious halt, just a pale shadow of its former importance. Gone are the days when a large fleet of crabbers braved the elements to scrape a living. The late Edgar Foster was born in 1901 and claimed to be the last crabber to go to sea in a clinker-built sailing boat, following in the sea boots of both his father and grandfather, each generation passing on the skills and tricks of the trade down the line. Edgar remembered an age when it was possible to put down thirty pots on West Rocks – about as many as could be managed between the tides – and not be surprised to have a haul of thirty lobsters. However, there were drawbacks, for although the sea was more plentiful, the limitations of the sailing boats of the early 1900s meant that if the wind was in the wrong direction it could take three backbreaking hours to reach the crab-pots. However, nature compensated for this by blowing the crabbers back to port in 45 minutes!

Another disadvantage of these boats was that they could be easily overturned and once in this position it was a fairly hopeless situation for their two-man crews. A tragic example of this occurred at Easter in 1898 following a particularly severe winter. Despite being under financial pressure, the men from these creeks always followed the time-honoured convention of not going to sea on Sundays or Good Friday – it was deemed as a sure bringer of bad luck or, worse, it would incur the wrath of the vicar! Unfortunately the inclement weather, which had prevented them from going to sea for a fortnight, relented on Good Friday and several fishermen decided to leave the safe haven of the Yealm to go fishing. Enough fish were caught to bait the crab pots and on Easter Monday morning most of the creek's fishermen set sail again. However, on passing Cellars Beach, most of them realised that the weather was once more taking a turn for the worse. Although there was little wind there was a big swell – evidence of a storm not that far away. Even as the men weighed up what their prospects were, the wind began to increase. Although some battled with the elements, most headed back to the shelter of the Pool. Two boats, each with a crew of two, persevered against all the odds but, sadly, all four men lost their lives that fateful day as the swell swamped their small boats.

In those long-gone days the fishermen were great improvisers, making a lot of the equipment that they used themselves, although the sails for their tiny craft were usually made at Plymouth. Edgar Foster recalled taking most of his catches to Plymouth by sea but occasionally they were taken up to the railway near Steer Point, at the head of the 'River Kitley'. (The Rev C. B. Yonge, the incumbent at the time, greatly disliked the use of this name instead of the River Yealm and suggested that the paddle steamer operators had introduced the name in ignorance of the true facts.) At Steer Point the catch was transferred to the branch railway, which ran from Yealmpton to Plymouth. The line opened in 1898 and was operated by the GWR from Yealmpton to Plymstock where it connected with the London & South Western line taking it to Friary station in Plymouth. This was just up the slope from the Barbican, where the catch would ultimately be sold. The line closed to passengers in July 1930 but re-opened during the Second World War to be in use from November 1941 to October 1947 when it again ceased working.

In the early years of the twentieth century coal was used by most people to heat their houses so it was obviously a much more important commodity than it is today. One Plymouth coal merchant was also aware of the inaccessibility of these twin villages so chose to bring the coal around to Newton and Noss by barge. Mashford Brothers navigated the shallows wherever they could, propelling their vessel with long poles, in a fashion resembling gondoliers. The brothers would travel all the way up the Newton Creek to Bridgend. Here they unloaded the coal into baskets, which would then be delivered by horse and cart around the villages. The whole exercise must have been extremely tiring, physical work.

In those early days there were always a dozen or so houseboats on the river, often occupied by ex-navy men who sought the continuing communion with a life on the water, Commander Davy being just one to spend several years here. Edgar Foster supplemented his income by using a punt to deliver bread and other items to these river people.

Just as it is today, the regatta was always the major event on the local calendar. On such occasions it was customary for several paddle steamers to visit the estuary, providing the perfect floating grandstands for spectators.

It is claimed that the 'Greyback Race' between Newton and Noss was established before the Oxford and Cambridge Boat Race, and there were certain parallels that would be obvious to those who have seen this titanic struggle between the two home-grown crews, one from each side of the creek. Originally the boats were crabbers as there were up to about forty of these craft working out of here at one time. However, whalers replaced them but still provided a wonderful spectacle. On page 32 we have a wonderful

picture of a past regatta – one can almost feel the atmosphere. One interpretation of the meaning of 'Greyback' was that these were the bare backs of farm workers who stripped off their shirts for the race. The Greyback races were staged up to the Second World War.

There have been, and remain, many light moments in the annual regatta. One race features pram dinghies, a vessel resembling a rectangular Welsh coracle, with blunt ends fore and aft. These are difficult craft to manoeuvre at the best of times but for the regatta the oarsmen are obliged to wear blindfolds! This causes great amusement to spectators – in the mayhem of the race most of the participants row around in dizzy, hopeless circles.

Today there are eight teams, these being made up of two senior and two junior teams from each village. Pride and rivalry are still vital elements as the villages do battle.

This maritime community became the first in Devon to get their own pair of racing gigs, thus providing many local people with the opportunity to race in the Scillies and at other places in Cornwall. The gigs are called *Hornet* and *Wasp* but are not involved in regatta races, needing more space in which to compete.

The inter-village rivalry extended to other aspects of creek life. Jack Crocker, a wonderful Noss Mayo character, was a child in the early 1900s. He recalls that if ever

he was ill and needed to see the doctor, who was in Newton Ferrers, that he would get his mother to take him as he would be too afraid to go by himself.

And this attitude wasn't one-sided – Jack also recalls how George, a member of the well-known Hockaday family, married and went to live in Noss. Bill Hockaday, his brother, remaining in Newton Ferrers, was obliged to go down to the water's edge and call out, as loudly as he could, "George, George, bring back the razor – I haven't had a scrape for a week!" – Bill wouldn't step into Noss territory!

There was also a rhyme, chanted by the boys of Noss Mayo, probably when the tide was in – "Newton Boys, Newton Boys, Sitting on the Quay, Come along a Strong Wind and Blow you out to Sea!" No doubt these words were borne on the wind but history doesn't relate what the response to it was.

Jack left school the same day that the First World War ended – could anyone possibly forget such an auspicious day? He later made his living as a rabbit trapper and stonemason and, after acquiring a plot of land, eventually built his own home on the side of the River Yealm. Having lived so long in such a close-knit community he was full of stories, some funny, others tragic. He told the tale of one of his relations, Joe Hartnell, who was a restless soul; in an age when most people found their niche and stuck with it he couldn't settle for one occupation, trying his hand at many jobs. He started by running the *Puffing Billy* ferry, carrying passengers up the 'Kitley River' (Yealm) to Steer Point, before he sold out to Mr Hodge. He tried his hand at other tasks like making crab pots, and selling fish. After a time in America he came home but fate wasn't kind to him. He returned to the river as a crabber but drowned in the estuary after his small craft capsized when he was out alone, his body being found in the river.

The *Kitley Belle* was a much-loved ferry, a familiar sight on the Yealm, run as a family business by the Messrs Hodge. In 1905 the crew of four comprised the Captain, George Hodge, the engineer, Ernest Hodge, the deck hand, George Hodge junior, and the general helper, Elliot Hodge.

However, paddle steamers, even small ones, were always prone to be heavy on fuel and when the General Strike of 1926 brought the country to its knees it proved the death knell for these coal-hungry vessels. One by one they disappeared from the scene, being replaced, albeit temporarily, by motor launches that were more economical by burning petrol. The *Alexandra* was typical, being built in 1888, lasting forty fruitful years before then being consigned to the scrapyard, in 1928, at Cattedown, Plymouth.

Through this glorious age the ships entering and leaving the mouth of the Yealm did so largely without incident. A lifeboat station was built in 1878 but in almost fifty years of service effected just four rescues. Over this span of five decades there were three lifeboats, the *Bowman*, the *Daring* and the *Michael Smart*. Local fisherman Harry Hockaday was the lifeboat coxswain for a long while, the Hockaday connection lasting throughout the time there was a lifeboat here. In fact the Hockadays are still around in strength. The lifeboat station closed in 1927 but we have this marvellous picture of the crew, complete with cork life jackets, as a visible reminder of their former existence.

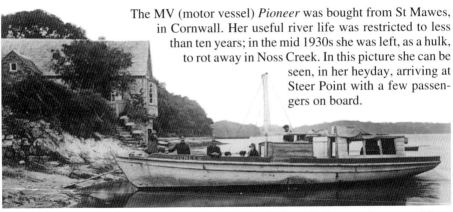

The MV (motor vessel) *Pioneer* was bought from St Mawes, in Cornwall. Her useful river life was restricted to less than ten years; in the mid 1930s she was left, as a hulk, to rot away in Noss Creek. In this picture she can be seen, in her heyday, arriving at Steer Point with a few passengers on board.

The 1920s was also the decade that saw the arrival of regular bus services to and from Plymouth so there was a drift away from travel by sea to inland mobility. Mr Hodge was an adaptable man and, with the demise of the river trade up to Steer Point, he stayed with the times and ran buses.

Travellers were still thirsty, whichever way they travelled, and the villagers had a choice of pubs in which to quench their thirsts. The Globe, now the Old Ship Inn, was a popular retreat after a long day in the salt air. In the 1920s and 30s the landlord, Henry Bidgood, kept a good house, his own children having enjoyable childhoods in this quiet haven, several boats being moored to the pub. A gig was also kept there. The Globe Inn took in a lot of summer visitors, not just families but also small-time writers and artists. It was quite common for some of these creative souls to book rooms for the whole season, year after year. The demand for cream teas also supplemented the family's income although these were not with scones but 'chudleys'– semi-sweet yeast buns. Other popular 'fayre' included whitebait suppers and lobster salads.

Charles Veale, a retired naval man, was an earlier tenant of the Globe. He had other interests and was not always at the inn when it was open. Sometimes a customer entering the bar would hear a call from Mrs Veale upstairs, "Help yourself!"

The River Yealm, a short river, at about 12 miles in length, starts high on nearby Dartmoor. Years ago it was a regular day out for people in this part of Devon to visit a beauty spot known as 'Hawns and Dendles' on the upper part of the river. This wonderful stretch of moorland Yealm, a series of plunging cascades, was open to the public on Mondays, Wednesdays and Saturdays in the 1920s and 30s by kind permission of the owner. During the First World War much of the timber from Hawns and Dendles Woods was removed for war purposes. Today it's private land, people are now denied access to the loveliness of this moorland-born river which plunges downwards over enormous rocks from off the heights of the moor. Downstream the Yealm passes anonymously beneath the A38 main Exeter to Plymouth road at Lee Mill, enjoys a few quiet miles down to Yealmpton and then starts to get more interesting again as it approaches its estuary at Kitley. A short way down river the small tributary of Silverbridge Lake, feeding Mudbank Creek, adds its flow and at Steer Point the Yealm is joined by Cofflete Creek which runs down from Brixton Torr.

The nature and number of these various estuarine creeks has meant that people travelling the roads in the district have had to go on lengthy detours. There are not many straight line journeys, the proverbial crow having a distinct advantage over the human race, which is obliged to travel over 'terra firma' and along the maze of roads needed to skirt these maritime inlets. From the church in Noss Mayo to Smeaton's Tower on Plymouth Hoe, the straight line distance is just a tad under six miles but to drive it is many miles farther. The situation is even more exaggerated when you note that Wembury's church of St Werburgh is, in a straight line, exactly two miles from that of Noss Mayo but a road distance of just under ten miles, even using short cuts and narrow lanes. However, on the plus side it serves to semi-isolate the Newton and Noss area, leaving it relatively undisturbed as it is almost on the road to nowhere. It was generally regarded, in Victorian and Edwardian times, as easier to get around by water, roads in this 'remote' corner of the county being more of a challenge than a joy to travel along.

Since 1928 the Yealm has been used as a testing station for International Paints Ltd,

a firm that produce paints primarily for the shipping industry. A marine biological research station was set up, although many yachtsmen have sailed by without knowing what was going on there. Rafts with plates descending in to the water were set up to test a range of different paints for their seaworthiness in terms of rust protection and stopping vessels from 'fouling' which, as a confirmed landlubber, I am informed is the crusting up of seagoing vessels by the various organisms, barnacles and the like, that attach themselves to boats.

The Yealm's estuary, a long-established Area of Outstanding Natural Beauty, extends southwards from Puslinch and Brixton for more than two miles and, apart from a few access points, the only way to enjoy or experience it is to be on the water. In the middle of the stretch of water known as Yealm Pool, or simply 'The Pool', which runs from above Misery Point up to Madge Point there is a coming together of inlets with the Newton Creek mingling its waters with that of the Yealm's.

Newton Ferrers peeps at the Yealm as it veers sharply from its general southward flow to bear westwards into the sea at Wembury Bay. The estuary, like almost every other one in the South West, has suffered from some water pollution. It's believed that there are not as many species of fish or numbers of fish as there were in the past when the water was bluey-black, thick with the enormous shoals of grey mullet that swam here, filling the river almost from bank to bank. They are still around but in greatly reduced numbers. Pollution has hit the maritime food chain so that a situation like this has evolved with less aquatic life.

The pub in Newton Ferrers is called the Dolphin, a good choice of name as a favourite sight of many villagers in the past was a school of bottle-nosed dolphins, chasing shoals of fish, which would be seen in these tidal inlets. However, there is still a healthy, tremendously varied flora and fauna in the area, particularly in the woods that line these estuaries so it's far from a gloom and doom situation. From time to time shoals of mackerel and scad would also swim up the creeks bringing many a local's supper, if not quite to the dinner table, almost to the door-step!

Whenever there is a sudden sharp increase in the population of a small place then problems usually occur with pollution. An influx of newcomers can have an adverse affect so it's not surprising that in the 1930s many locals watched in horror as things started to change here, with the contours of the hills greeting new residential roads.

The Devon Branch of the Council for the Preservation of Rural England engaged W. Harding Thompson to survey the coast, moors and rivers of the county in 1932. This was his brief assessment of Newton and Noss:

"These two villages, secreted on opposite sides of a winding creek off the Yealm, have become better known since the frequent bus service was established to Plymouth, for it is only recently that the road approach via Yealmpton has improved. Only a few of the inhabitants still carry on the occupation of their forefathers as fishermen, but most of the cottages survive from the seventeenth and eighteenth centuries; these are closely built on the steep hillsides of the creek that now affords a haven for smaller craft than formerly, owing to the gradual silting up of the channel. So far there has been little use of incongruous materials, and the grey slate and thatch roofs of the older cottages give

to the place an atmosphere something akin to the best of the Cornish fishing villages. Above Newton Ferrers there is a considerable amount of building land for sale with commanding views of the river; anything built in this conspicuous position will seriously affect the landscape unless of harmonious colour. The woodlands which clothe the banks of the Yealm are essential to the beauty of this river, and it would be of great advantage, therefore, if the landowners on both sides could co-operate in preventing any increase in the number of temporary structures that have been erected in the woods above the Coastguard Station.

"The valley above the Newton creek is serene and unspoilt, and the small village green near the old church forms an attractive approach from Yealmpton."

The creeks in the vicinity of Newton and Noss are a yachtsman's paradise. To give you a small insight into what life on the water may be like, for some, I have included a brief extract from *Under Sail Through South Devon & Dartmoor*, in my opinion the best book ever written about South Devon's coastline. Ray Cattell saw it in the mid 1930s, when he was about thirty years old, travelling in a small two-seater canoe-type craft that could take a sail. This excerpt from his 'masterpiece' begins at Gara Point, near the mouth of the Yealm, where he and his partner had been spending some time in a beautiful cove at the base of the cliffs, in the lee of this headland.

The coves appeared to be seldom or never visited (which hardly surprised me) for we found endless supplies of driftwood. For some reason driftwood, in spite of its years of immersion in salt water, will burn very fiercely, giving an intensely hot fire such as is never obtained with ordinary wood. On one cove we found a complete five course dinner, consisting of grapefruit, dogfish, bird, joint and a half-empty demijohn of rum – assembled there by the recent north-easterly breeze and the queer coincidence of tidal currents.

From our new home we caught the first glimpses of the coast of Cornwall – Rame Head – and as the blue night spread over land and sea we picked out the flash of the Eddystone far to the southwest.

Towards Plymouth, ships' lights come and go. The moon rises and sinks again, the stars gleam and fade, but the little window of our tent witnesses from dusk to dawn the constant heartbeat of the Eddystone's silvery gleam.

Lovely Gara; a pale green shadow of land making its home in the breezy blue sea: best of both elements, wild and unspoilt yet gentle and inviting. When it welcomed us from our ordeal by exhaustion along that iron coast I had felt like that ancient mariner who greeted the land with 'I have come to live and die here'. And the morning brought us no change of sentiment.

The Yealm was expecting us, but though we were so near we let the day go by. On the hills above we found blackberries bigger than we had ever seen before and these we combined with cream from Worswell Farm to make food of the gods. What a pleasant contrast in its quiet order and prosperity is Worswell ... and how naturally we were made to feel at home there.

On the following day the south-wester blew quite stiffly. In our sheltered cove we could almost feel the waves thudding on the other side of the thin headland. I have described how watchful of the weather we were at every point of our trip lest we should get stormbound on some open part of the cliff. Storms might rage when we had gained an estuary where we could still enjoy calm water sailing, but we were determined not to be pinned against a rocky coast. Yet here we were in an exposed position and the south-wester was momentarily strengthening.

We could not enter the Yealm till the afternoon for the tide was streaming out until then, but we were so near, only half a mile from shelter, that I swore we would go there whatever the sea. And go we did, though we had to fight our way around Gara Point in a most boisterous sea. Being well rested and near our goal we tackled this violent sea with the utmost zest, giving blow for blow and smashing our way successfully through ferocious blue billows which would certainly have given us a complete sinking feeling at other times. Beyond the Mewstone a cluster of twelve-metre yachts crossing in a smother of foam reminded us that we were approaching Plymouth in regatta time.

The Yealm in its upper reaches is a very beautiful wooded river like the Erme but at the last bend towards the sea, where the Noss Mayo creek runs off, the woods are cut away to make room for bungalows, good and bad, and the yachting colony of Noss. There were many lovely yachts moored here and one of them apparently had on board a troop of chorus girls. Any yachtsman who finds another spending his time moored in a creek immediately suspects him of harbouring chorus girls, or goes about darkly saying "Cherchez la femme". Women and the deep sea are apparently deadly enemies and there are no more adventurous beings than the men who live between the two. To judge by appearances these yachting men had agreed among themselves to say no more about the sea.

Noss Mayo creek is very interesting, if only because of the keen rivalry and separatism between Noss on one side of the creek and Newton on the other, said to be due to the former being a Celtic settlement and the latter Anglo-Saxon. Be that as it may, they are at present similar in being villages with more boatmen to the square yard than you will find anywhere along this coast. Every cottage seems to have its own landing stage, and the boats' painters pass in even through the bedroom windows, presumably being tied to the bedstead or the toe of some sleeping yachtsman.

Except for one or two mouldering stone ruins and a pretty group of houses by the ferry, there is practically nothing to interrupt the soft sweep of the wooded hills which flank the whole of the tidal Yealm and its creeks upstream. It is a scene wholly natural and sweet. One can see above the woods the far grey tors of Dartmoor.

Following the last creek, with a still running tide to help us, we came to the park-like grounds of an old country house – a beautifully proportioned Georgian house, modified in style by a mansard roof – a house looking as if it had once known rich and liberal times but now with half its rooms closed down. An old man, with fishing gear, who was mooring his boat as we arrived, proved to be the owner. Not only did he give us permission, in an old-world fashion, to make use of his grounds, but he walked down half an hour later to point out that the place we had chosen to camp would be flooded by the spring tide. It seemed incredible, for we were on a high grassy bank among trees, but that night the water came to within an inch of the mark he had made for us on a tree and to within two inches of the floor of our tent. And in the chilly dawn I saw swans swimming where the peak of our tent would have been.

Ray Cattell and his friend left behind the Yealm that day to carry on the voyage around the coast of Devon, a journey that occupied several summers. Years later he went on to become on of the world's greatest psychologists, working in the Mid-west of the USA before retiring to Hawaii where he was still hale and hearty when this book was being written, some three score years after his visit to the Yealm.

The house, in whose grounds Ray Cattell camped, was Puslinch, much nearer to Yealmpton than Newton Ferrers. The original house was some 200 yards to the west of the one that Cattell admired. It's believed that the same anonymous Plymouth mason was instrumental in designing three similar houses, the other two being at Plympton and at Anthony, just beyond the Tamar, in Cornwall.

Whoever he was, he is believed to have had a good teacher in Sir Christopher Wren.

When this early Georgian house, in the Queen Anne style, was built for James Yonge in 1718, the workforce set up their builders' yard in an adjacent field known as The Wilderness, the bricks being made in another field now aptly called Kiln Park. The strange name of Puslinch derives from the owners of the original house who owned it for three generations from 1300, their name being Poschynche. The house's name has undergone change throughout the years; various spellings include Puselynch, Posse-Linch (which sounds like something out of a cowboy film!), and my favourite, Puzzlewitch!

The surname synonymous with this lovely house is Yonge, and at the time when this house was built the family 'trade' was that of a surgeon; James Yonge was a naval surgeon, as his father and grandfather had been before him. The house has had its share of noted visitors. One of them was Charlotte M. Yonge (1823–1901), the Victorian novelist, best-known for *The Heir of Redclyffe* and other tearjerkers based on family life and influenced by a High Church philosophy. She would frequently travel down to Devon in the yellowish family chariot to stay with her uncle and aunt.

There are some other fine houses beside the Yealm. One is a striking, Spanish-looking,

villa called 'Casa Del Rio', well named for this means 'House of the River'. The original owner, Mr Price, whose family had made 'a lot of dough' out of being a leading bread manufacturer, had gone to Hollywood in the early 1930s. Whilst there he saw Mary Pickford's house and fell in love with it. He employed an architect to create a similar edifice and this was the result, the house being built in 1936 on the steep hillside above the Yealm. For those who are too young to remember, and that includes me, Mary Pickford (1893–1979), whose real name was a less glamorous-sounding Gladys Smith, was a Canadian actress from the days of the silent movies. She was known as 'the world's sweetheart'.

A house on the opposite side of the river, a short way up river, called 'Thorn' was originally owned by the Preston-born inventor Mr Richard Arkwright (1732–1792) of cotton-spinning fame, and thereby hangs the thread for he was a great traveller and brought back many exotic plants and shrubs from New Zealand and China whilst on his globe-trotting adventures. Some of these did well and thrived in this sheltered location. A few hundred yards upstream of Thorn is a low wall. In the past this allowed the rising tide to pass through a gate in it, ponding back the waters and the fish behind it. As the waters slowly emptied back into the estuary the fish were caught, thus providing an excellent source of food for the local populace. The 1:25 000 OS Map shows the course of the channel which issued from it, a location favoured by fishermen after silver bass.

In the 1930s another author, A. K. Wickham, penned a book called *The Villages of England*. Bearing in mind how many villages there are in this country, only a small proportion got a specific mention and those that were featured only received scant coverage – Newton Ferrers was one of them! With a somewhat disapproving air he wrote: "A recent photograph in a London newspaper, advertising 'Where to winter in England' reveals a post war [First World War] growth of villas and bungalows on these, the Yealm's, banks. This is unfortunately the case with most of the South Devon coast."

Whilst we are in that safe haven of quotes, a short time later the local vicar bemoaned some of the changes he had witnessed over his years of service here. In 1938 the Rev C. B. Yonge wrote *A Short History of Newton Ferrers* and had this to say on his last page (page 8) of the state of things as he saw it then.

"Old Newton is fast disappearing. Anybody who is over fifty years old can remember when there was no house west of Elm Tree Cottage on the low level, or Court on the higher level, except the house that Lord Revelstoke built on Newton Quay after he had purchased the Court Estate. But when he sold it again, about 43 years ago [1895], it was quickly divided up into building lots with the result that all the houses between the village and the harbour, high on the hill or low down near the creek, have been built. But not only is old Newton being surrounded by modern buildings, the old village itself is losing by degrees much of its ancient appearance. The picturesque stone stiles have given place to iron swing gates, the old thatched roofs to slate ones, the old stepping stones of the Foss have given place to a continuous concrete path. The Brook running between the slate washing slabs where the village women used to scrub their husbands' trousers has been covered in. All the more desirable is it to preserve ancient features which in no way are a hindrance to modern improvement. There is one old relic of the past which I hope may be allowed to remain, both as a token of the ancient past and for its own sake. The place in the village which is still called 'the Cross' has the old base of the village cross still there. The Parish Council have erected a lamp standard in the socket which was made for the cross to stand in. In its turn the standard has become a support for a notice board.

"I should like to see the Cross standing there once again in the midst of the village houses, as it must have stood for centuries. I am not one of those who believe it would be a sacred thing in danger of disrespect. We missed one opportunity of restoring it when

we decided to place the war memorial in the Churchyard; that was the general wish; though I think it would have been quite as fitting to have placed it at 'the Cross'."

Michael Ashton spent four impressionable and formative years growing up at Newton Ferrers in the late 1940s and like many who 'passed through' still has a soft spot for the area. Some of his fond recollections have been mingled into this book. For him those memories live on. One of his prized possessions is a painting by Tom Edridge who then lived in Court Road. Tom was a man of many talents who was also a writer and a radio broadcaster who fielded gardening questions and gave gardening tips.

In the 1940s there were two ferrymen who carried people between Newton and Noss when the tide was in but moved down to The Pool when it was out. Here they joined 'Pop' Carter and his son who ran the ferry from just below the Yealm Hotel. At that time and on the other side of the pier, where the old lifeboat house was located, there was another ferry operator, making at least five ferrymen vying for the cross-creek trade to either the Wembury or the Noss side of the inlets. On Bank Holidays even five ferrymen could not cope with the demand and schoolboys, like young Michael Ashton, were pressed into service, working flat out from 9.00 a.m. to 6.00 p.m. On those occasions when Michael went up the Yealm he never failed to notice the sad 'wreck' of the *Kitley Belle* rotting in the mud near Kitley.

Another 'Pop' was an Irishman, 'Pop' Hosford, shown here outside 'Barnicott',who was a deeply religious man, nothing distracting him from his bible reading. When Michael Ashton's father took him

some precious 'Black Market' butter he would utter, "Thank you," but not look up or interrupt his intense scrutiny of the Good Book!

The milkman in Newton Ferrers at that time was Mr Kingcombe, who doled out milk to his customers' jugs using a ladle. Meanwhile a village baker did his rounds in the morning and then used the same van to collect pig swill in the afternoon. And where would you go in those halcyon days for a haircut? That's right – the garage!

There were one or two unusual characters in the district. The Gilberts were a pair of retired schoolmasters whose claim to fame was that Sir Alec Guinness, as a child, had been a pupil at their private school.

The village has also housed some real treasures. In 1950 there were at Court House (which had just undergone a complete renovation) some unique pieces of furniture. There was a chair regularly used by Sir Francis Drake and also a portrait of him. There was the table where Napoleon sat to sign his abdication and the history theme continued with a portrait of Nelson, and another of an early member of the de Ferrers family.

The twin villages have a church each, both beautifully located and topographically balanced, so that when seen from a distance they look like a matching pair. As Newton Ferrers' is much the older, we will start with a brief look at the Church of the Holy Cross, where the presence of the stocks is an indication that not all the residents were law-abiding in the past. The last person to be ensconced within them was in 1850, just a decade under two hundred years after they had been first purchased. Whilst his master was worshipping at church, one despicable man was guilty of stealing his master's hens. However, he was caught, placed in the stocks at the entrance and also obliged to purchase penny buns, which he then had to give to everyone coming to church that day. The 'sentence' had been devised by the parish constable who also just happened to be the village baker, who sold the villain the buns!

A look at the list of serving vicars at Holy Cross reveals that the name Yonge is a frequent one, there being an almost continuous run between 1752 and 1938. The name has already been mentioned in association with Puslinch and this was once part of the manor of Newton Ferrers. With it went the right of presentation to the living of that parish.

This is a brief excerpt from a detailed newspaper article written on the eve of the reopening of the church following a major refurbishment, completed in 1893:

"Newton Ferrers' fine old church is dedicated to the Holy Cross, and boasts of a grand and venerable grey western tower that  *frowns a sort of grim challenge across the creek to the rugged rocks on the other side, whereupon is perched, in almost equal regal dignity, the sumptuous church of St Peter the Fisherman, which the earnest piety and princely liberality of the Baroness and Lord Revelstoke induced them to build a few years ago, and give to the simple cotters of their estate at Revelstoke and at Noss Mayo to worship forever.*

"Tomorrow his lordship of Exon, in his episcopal capacity as Lord Bishop of the Diocese, will be present to re-dedicate and to reopen the fine old church after a very careful and costly renovation."

In early December 1946 the residents of Newton Ferrers, and probably those of Noss Mayo, may have thought that the war had started all over again, such were effects of a thunderstorm of great intensity which struck in an awesome show of blazing light and fearful loud bangs. Holy Cross in Newton Ferrers received a direct hit, the storm singling out the flagstaff rather than the intentionally-placed, purpose-built lightning conductor. The flagstaff was turned into matchwood and was unrecognisable as to what it had been prior to the strike. The blast that hit the tower of the church was spectacular, sending its force through the fabric of the building. One of the church's pinnacles was ripped off and parts of it were found a quarter of a mile away! The full force of the impact was passed down through the tower, so that two stout, locked oak doors were blasted off their hinges and flung yards into the churchyard. A glass and wood screen, that served to divide the interior of the church from that of the tower, was smashed to bits. However, despite the damage to the building, the clock and the bells remained unharmed and intact.

One villager, who watched in awe as these wild natural elements held sway, described the lightning show as just 'like a thousand stars', such was the magnitude of the storm at its height. There was something of a rude awakening for all those who had gone to the institute for the weekly film show. They, along with everyone else in the district, were plunged into sudden darkness, the power supply being cut off in an instant. The film-goers had to leave the dark hall and make their way home before the outcome of the film was known.

Noss Mayo's church, high on the other side of the creek, escaped the storm's attentions. It's a beautiful church, as we have already seen, paid for by Mr Edward Charles Baring, much more of whom we will hear later on.

The laying of the foundation stone was a well attended affair for it coincided with the village harvest festival. The dignitaries watched the proceedings from a special platform covered by an awning. Parishioners knew that the gesture of paying for such a grand edifice was an incredible one so collected a large sum of money to buy a silver trowel, level and mallet for Mrs Baring to perform the task. These articles were of beautiful workmanship, the woodwork being from the old parish church, a circumstance which Mr Roe, the kind-hearted and earnest rector, alluded to in his address. They were all engraved with the Baring coat of arms and upon the trowel was the following inscription: 'The offering of Revelstoke and Membland to Mrs Edward Baring, when she placed this corner stone of St Peter's Church, Revelstoke, September 1880.' The articles were supplied by Messrs Page, Keen and Page of Plymouth.

The day's weather forecast hadn't been too promising but the mist lifted and, although it was overcast, it didn't rain. Some spectators travelled from Plymouth on the 'good steamer *Empress*'.

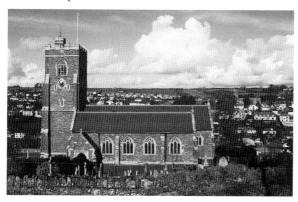

As in the refit of Newton Ferrers' church, some of the top local craftsmen were engaged in the building and furnishing of the new St Peter's. Mr Baring was anxious that the work should be given to local firms in preference, whenever practicable, to those from farther afield. Nothing was scrimped as architect Mr James Piers St Aubyn oversaw the careful construction of the church, about 100 feet in length and some 50 feet wide. Apart from the more intricate work the church was built entirely by Mr Baring's own estate workers under the supervision of Samuel W. Adams. The resident clerk of the works was George Crosbie.

The exquisite windows and other decorations were completed by Messrs Fouracres and Watson of Stonehouse, Plymouth. The marble inlays were done by Mr Gullett of Yealmpton, and the sculptured fittings were created by that genius of church works, Harry Hems of Exeter. One clever touch was the depiction, in the corner of one of the sculptured bench ends, which apparently represents a sea battle from Elizabethan times, when the Barings were involved in a conflict with the Spanish. This carving has been inscribed: "Harry Hems and his merrie men carved all these benches at Exeter, AD 1882."

This was typical of this master craftsman, whose former workplace is now a restaurant called 'Harry's' in Longbrook Street, but if you pay a visit just look at the wonderfully ornate nature of his 'factory'!

Two years later this fine church, which cost something in the region of £30,000, was opened, a major event in the parish's history. Many local dignitaries attended this proud occasion, the guest list reading like a 'Who's Who?' of all the well-known people from south west Devon. The church was so packed that many were left outside. The villages of Newton and Noss were both crowded with visitors as a fleet of steamers had sailed in from Plymouth for this great day.

After the service specially invited guests repaired to Membland Hall, home of the Barings, for a superb lunch that was provided by Mr Mallett of Ivybridge.

Jack Crocker's relation, Elizabeth Crocker, died just nine days before the church was opened. Her funeral was delayed until the first grave could be dug for her in the new churchyard, Lady Revelstoke kindly paying for this first plot to be filled.

The Swinging Sixties meant other things in Newton and Noss. When the Beatles were first tearing up the charts the parishioners of the two churches were steeling themselves ready for change. There had been a shortage of vicars and the church was going through something of a lean time having to rationalise where possible. In 1962, a short time after the Rev H. W. T. Stamp had arrived to take charge at Holy Cross, the Rector of Revelstoke, the Rev G. R. Channer, died suddenly. Here was an opportunity to make savings and, with the approval of the Church Commissioners, the Rev. Stamp became the first rector of both churches.

However, we have to go back more than a century to what many people consider to be the golden era for this neighbourhood, when the rich and famous graced this corner of the Devonshire landscape. The hamlet of Membland is not very far from the twin villages of Newton and Noss and, as we have already briefly seen, has had a tremendous influence on life in this quiet part of the county and in many far-flung corners of the world! Money and influence invariably go hand in hand and the Squire of Noss Mayo, the proud owner of Membland Hall, was a man of enormous wealth who fell firmly into this category, that is until his famous firm hit a rocky patch, a situation that was to repeat itself a century later with devastating consequences.

Some of Devon's greatest families have had their links with Membland, an ancient place mentioned in the Domesday Book as 'Mimilande'. By the time of Edward I the manorial rights belonged to the Hillersden family, the first Manor House being built in 1272. Various owners included the celebrated Champernownes, the Bulteels and also Sir John Pering, Lord Mayor of London.

Perhaps the lanes of Membland were themselves paved with gold for Mr Edward Charles Baring, of banking fame, who married Louisa Emily Charlotte Bulteel of Flete, bought the Membland estate in 1877. The fact that it had once belonged to his wife's family probably had some bearing, if you'll excuse the pun, on the decision to purchase the property.

The family had long-standing connections with Devon, particularly with Exeter where there are still roads named after this great family. In the 1850s the company of Baring Bros & Co. was run by Thomas Baring and Henry Mildmay, another well-known name in this corner of Devon. The latter was a nephew and son-in-law of Alexander Baring and had been created Lord Ashburton in 1835.

The firm was later controlled by Edward Charles Baring, who was Thomas Baring's nephew, and Henry Bingham Mildmay, who was Henry's son. He bought the Flete Estate, so most of the land between the rivers Yealm and Erme was owned by someone from this banking clan.

Mr E. C. Baring later acquired his own title when, in 1885, he became Lord Revelstoke. The name is an old one and goes back to the days of Richard I when another Richard, this time Revell, was the Sheriff of Devon. He owned much property here and chose it as the place for his residence.

Mr Baring spent a fortune on 'improvements' at Membland. The Hall took on a completely new appearance in those years around 1880 with the addition of a tower and a new east wing. Many said that the Hall had been made into a much more comfortable place in which to live but the various extensions did not enhance the overall appearance of the house. But that was not the end of it for added to this there were many more attractive buildings constructed in and around this immediate area of this growing hamlet. His additions to the area not only included the new church for Noss Mayo, but also a post office, school and lodges. By the time all the various additions had been established Membland was virtually a self-contained village in its own right. The standard colour for all the buildings was 'Revelstoke Blue', an early form of corporate identity! There were also vast improvements to roads and bridges so that getting around was made easier for the local populace.

For his own comfort Edward added an indoor tennis court, which was also used for grand balls and the Christmas party when the house was filled to the rafters with guests. There was also a cricket pitch, complete with pavilion, and a superb billiards room which made the place into the Victorian equivalent of a leisure centre, except that the guests were non-paying and only from the elite of society. Some of the world's finest musicians passed through the portals of this splendid sanctuary, so far from the madding crowd. What better place could there have been to relax and recharge?

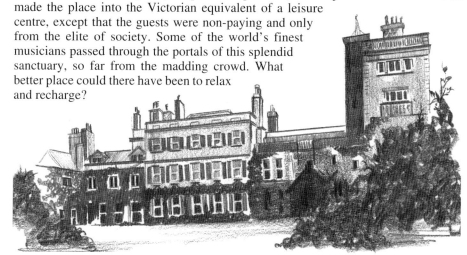

The rich and the famous were regular visitors to this lovely part of Devon. The Prince of Wales, later to become Edward VII, the Czar of Russia, Baron Rothschild and Gladstone were just a quartet of visitors who enjoyed their time at Membland. It's been suggested that the Prince of Wales may well have brought his 'friend' Lily Langtree to savour the delights of the Devon countryside, away from the gaze of the media, a far less potent force in those days. There were many other household names of that Victorian and Edwardian era who travelled to Devon to be treated with the most hospitable welcome that could ever be imagined. The famous Rev. Sabine Baring-Gould, the vicar of Lewtrenchard in West Devon, author of 'Onward Christian Soldiers' and re-discoverer of the Widecombe anthem about Uncle Tom Cobley, was also a regular guest. A beautiful organ was installed so that he could play when he was there, nothing being too much trouble to keep everyone happy.

When King Edward VII's Coronation was to be celebrated, an invitation was extended to all the villagers of Newton and Noss to come to Membland Hall and to enjoy games, sports and dancing, this to the musical accompaniment of a concertina. George V, when he was Prince of Wales, was another visitor to Membland, the first man to be seen driving a car in the twin villages. It must have been blissful motoring in those days!

Some came by sea in their sumptuous yachts. The inlet of the Yealm was an excellent sheltered anchorage and the clifftop carriageway from there to the house was something very special, the most stunning of rides. It has been said, but never proved, that it was built as there was a possibility that Queen Victoria might honour Membland with her presence, something that never transpired. It was built by local fishermen who were employed out of season, a symbiotic relationship that gave them extra income and provided Lord Revelstoke with a magnificent, nine miles long carriageway contouring the cliffs of a spectacular coastline.

That wonderful carriageway is now such a stunning coastal walk for all to explore and enjoy. It's believed that Lord Revelstoke's children had a truly happy childhood here and Maurice, one of his sons, who himself achieved great things in a sphere other than banking and high finance, and in a wider world, wrote fondly of his formative years in his autobiography *The Puppet Show of Memory*.

The Barings produced a total of nine children but one, Rupert, died in infancy and is buried at St Peter the Poor Fisherman at Revelstoke – but we'll get to that unique church later. Margaret (1868–1906) was one of the daughters. She married Charles Robert Spencer and could never have conceived what fate her union would have had on the history of our country in the late twentieth century, for one of her great grandchildren became the Princess of Wales.

Apart from enjoying the journey along the cliff-top carriageway, the Barings also loved travelling on the water. The *Waterwitch*, their 150-ton schooner, was a regular participant at Cowes week. Their other acquisition was a steam launch, the *Wasp*, often used for the journey to Plymouth, where 'cook' purchased the supplies needed to run this amazing household.

There was an impressive boathouse and there were also stores for fish catches, again built by Lord Revelstoke. The locals also used this facility, known as Baulking House Stores, to keep and process their catches. From time to time visiting French fishing vessels also used it to handle and package their own catches, these being mainly of lobster and crab. It was also likely that a significant amount of French brandy was smuggled into this inlet.

The Barings' banking activities extended across the world. Just one example was the Canadian Pacific Railway who were pioneering routes through that great mountain range, the Rockies. At a crucial stage, when the railroad from the east was to be united with that being forged from the west, the company had run out of money so Barings stepped in to finance the completion of the venture. As a token of the CPR's gratitude, in 1899 a newly-created railway town was named 'Revelstoke'. This has become a popular tourist resort in the Mount Revelstoke National Park. If you want to find it in your atlas it's on the banks of the mighty River Columbia, just above Upper Arrow Lake in British Columbia. Its latitude is precisely 51° north (similar to Revelstoke, Devon which is just a shade over 50° north) and 118° west. It is surrounded by towering mountains.

However, in the world of business there are other 'peaks' and, unfortunately for Lord Revelstoke, troughs. Problems mounted for the Barings in the 1890s when they amassed liabilities of more than twenty million pounds. Although they had securities in South America, economic conditions militated against these being able to bail them out of their deep predicament. Fortunately Barings had many contacts in the world of finance and a rescue package was put together in great haste. This involved the Banks of England and France and many other leading financiers. This time Barings was saved but at a cost. Consequently this temporary, but spectacular, slump in the family fortunes forced Lord Revelstoke to sell the village of Noss Mayo. However, the firm survived this particular crisis because of the guarantee fund that was set up almost overnight.

The first Lord Revelstoke died in 1897, having survived his wife by five years, and the estate was sold to a business syndicate from London. They didn't hold onto it for long, Sir William Cresswell Gray, a wealthy shipbuilder from Hartlepool, becoming the next owner. He didn't show a lot of interest in his new acquisition, choosing only to come down to Membland in summer, mainly to shoot. It was not uncommon for his shooting parties to bag between 500 and 600 birds in a single shoot, so the bird population of the neighbourhood was never that pleased when the tycoon was around!

Poaching was rife in a district containing so much game worth shooting. However, it demanded a wily soul to become involved in this illegal practice because the consequences of being caught could be far-reaching. It was not unknown for men living in rented accommodation to be evicted from their homes for one indiscretion in this matter.

There were many 'keepers' to keep a lookout on those who might try their luck in the hope of making a 'quick killing'. George Baker (pictured here) was head-gardener at Membland.

During the First World War the decaying estate was taken over by the military who set up a training camp there for training leaders. As you might expect the officers slept in the house whilst the soldiers camped in the grounds. They knew their place! However, many of them were from leading universities and public schools, hand-picked for later heroics. For many of them it was their last experience of life in England. The 'No 1 Officers' Cadet Battalion', with Lieut. Col. Arthur Trueman in command, produced many such men from their two companies at Membland. They also installed a third company at nearby Alston Hall.

The training was not a case of all work and no play and from lunch time on Saturday to Monday morning the trainee officers could escape the disciplined regime to enjoy

themselves. Cars were virtually nonexistent and Membland was a remote outpost. To 'get back to civilisation' the young men marched down to the small wooden pier at Noss Mayo. Here they could catch the *Kitley Belle* to Steer Point. Another short walk up the road saw the officers arrive at the station on the branch line which ran to the heart of Plymouth. It's believed that the same route was taken back to Membland, the main discernible difference being the boisterous nature of the young men who had, perhaps, been enjoying a last taste of the good life. No one, not even the ferrymen, would have begrudged those young men these pleasures. Some say that they can still hear their raucous ghostly singing on still nights...

Their Commander, Lieut. Col. Trueman, survived the war having been involved in much of the early action of this great conflict. He had married Miss Victoria Bewes who hailed from nearby Gnaton Hall. Alas, this much-loved and highly-respected hero and his wife both caught pneumonia, just after the cessation of hostilities, and both died.

There was an exciting incident to punctuate the humdrum life of those who lived at Newton and Noss in those First World War days. One vessel to anchor in Yealm Pool was called the *Egret*. Her owner was arrested in a daring raid for he turned out to be a German spy!

Newton Ferrers and Noss Mayo

After the end of the First World War, Membland Hall was put on the market again, it having been also put on offer, yet again, in July 1915, but this time it proved to be something of a white elephant and nobody wanted it.

There were many happy householders and farmers who realised their dreams in a 1921 grand sell-off. Locals saw it as an opportunity to buy their own rented property and raised the finance to do so. Properties that were sold included Pool Mill Dairy, Pool Mill Farm and Post Office Farm. The Plymouth Co-operative Wholesale Society, a go-ahead concern, also seized the opportunity to make some astute buys. In fact one of the last major events to be staged at Membland Hall was the Plymouth Co-operative Society's staff dance.

However Membland Hall was eventually bought in 1924 only to be demolished some four years later. Mr Stanley Pitts acquired the Hall, cottages, lodge houses, stables and 227 acres of land.

When it was realised that the threat of demolishing the Hall was a reality strong protests were made. A locally-produced leaflet was printed and circulated to those who might be able to convert it into a useful building such as a school, a hotel or a retirement home but there were no takers. There was then the sorry episode of the demolition sale at the hall. Following this the building was dynamited so that roof timbers and beams and any useful recyclable materials could be taken away. The house lay in ruins for some thirty years. However, like the phoenix rising from the ashes, the old ruins, that had been such a fine playground for the children of the area for years, saw stirrings in 1960. Mr Bradford, whose family had enjoyed regular holidays in this area over a span of years, bought the site of the ruins and what little there was left of the tower was demolished to make way for a new house, started in 1966 and finished some two years later, on top of the old foundations. And so it was that Membland House appeared, almost as if by magic, to replace the previous imposing building. The former covered tennis court, where the Christmas parties were enjoyed with such enthusiasm, has been converted into flats.

It is strongly recommended that anyone new to the area, on holiday or recently becoming a resident here, should do the following walk which, for the most part, uses Lord Revelstoke's carriageway or 'The Nine Mile Drive'. Without reservation I would say that this is one of the most enjoyable walks in Devon, and this is in a county blessed by many opportunities for some superb strolls. Although it uses the carriageway, this walk is not quite nine miles long.

The walk begins at Bridgend where the creek comes to a sudden end, just like so many others in the South Hams. Parking is always a problem in these twin villages so you will need to find a spot where you do not impede local traffic.

If it's a sunny morning you will notice that Newton Ferrers has the advantage of facing south, therefore soaking up the more direct heat of the sun's warmth. What a great location it would be for a vineyard!

Head south westwards along the road towards Noss Mayo but before you get into

Newton Ferrers in the 1950s

your stride, just before the first buildings on your right, turn left onto a steep 'No Through Road'. This is Hewster's Hill and will be your corridor for almost a mile. The first part of the road is surfaced up to a hillside property but soon twists sharply left turning into a rough track. The initial, sometimes slippery, steepness, the toughest bit of the whole walk, only lasts for about 400 yards but provides two consolations. The first is that the heights attained give great views, from a gateway on the right, straight down the creek and the second is that once you have scaled the steep slope the going becomes decidedly easier, the improving lane picking out a ridge route of sorts. The only drawbacks lie in a few hollows in the path where, in the wet monsoon season, enormous puddles add an aquatic theme to the walk. Sometimes it's best just to roll up the trouser legs, throw caution to the wind and plough through. This technique is not nearly so bad as it sounds for it is often the case that the nimble-footed wayfarer who skirts the edge of such watery obstacles slips into the obstacle, landing with a mighty splash that is far worse than a 'high-tide' mark just above the ankles. However, you may be blessed by dry conditions underfoot. The lane rises past the buildings of Great Prideaux, on your left, the road now being surfaced.

It ends at a T-junction with the road that runs from the coast through the hamlet of Membland and back to Bridgend. When we reach it we turn right to head along the neatly hedge-clipped lane to the coast, leaving Membland and all its late Victorian history way behind. Many famous folk have been along the route that we are now following, so if it was good enough for them it's good enough for us!

Soon Tea House Cross is reached where the sign points left to Plymouth, 14 miles, when geographically it's far more to the right, if anything. All we have to do to reach the cliff-tops is traipse straight ahead along over a green causeway across the field onto the famous 'Nine Mile Drive' at Beacon Hill. Suddenly route instructions become simplicity itself for the drive leads the way, no place encountered where one's life is threatened by a plunge from a precipitous promontory if the path is followed. All you have to do is soak up the atmosphere, relax and savour this terrific coastal walk. One possible 'cloud on the horizon' is the phantom traveller of this former carriageway, the ghost of someone called Peter Perrin who, apparently, played a part in the downfall of the Barings late-nineteenth century dynasty. Ghostly carriages have also been seen trundling along the track but you will know what they are when you see them, for they have a habit of disappearing into thin air as they reach you, unlike mountain bikes!

Had you been doing this walk in the Spring of 1995 you might have been excused for thinking that you had seen this ghostly carriage because a scene for the wonderful screen version of Jane Austen's *Sense and Sensibility* was shot farther along here, the carriage trundling around a bend with the obvious landmark of the Great Mew Stone in the distance giving the game away as to where it was. Much of the rest of the film was filmed at Mothecombe and the Erme estuary just a bit farther east along the coast.

At the ruin of the Tea House, high on top of Beacon Hill, there is a grand view along the coast. Away to the east is the unusual outcrop of St Anchorite's Rock with the mouth of the Erme beyond. If the weather is clear Burgh Island can be spied farther along the Bigbury Bay shoreline. In the other direction the caravan park at Stoke Beach can be seen. The Tea House was built for the benefit of the Baring family and their guests, a place for refreshments. Jack Crocker, of Noss Mayo, remembers the building before it became a target of vandals. He used to hang his rabbits up here and whilst doing so enjoyed the views out of the windows, strategically placed to enjoy the scenic views. It was never a tea house open to the public.

Way down below the carriageway are a number of small inlets, the largest of these being Piskey's Cove, the remote location ideal for our little friends of folklore fame to live in peace and splendid isolation near the wave-battered rocks on the storm-kissed shores. The carriageway affords an easy passage as it wends its way to Stoke. An avenue of trees, contorted into a regimented, slanted position by the sea breeze, some people saying that they have 'always been that way inclined', is passed through just before meeting a road by the visitors' car park at the top of the hill above the Stoke Beach Caravan Park.

If you have never visited this place before it's worth a detour down the long slope through the caravan park to visit the former parish church of Noss Mayo. In the past it was not unusual to site such places so far from their congregations. It may have been done as a landmark for shipping, a feature to help them know their whereabouts, perhaps. This ruined church, which Ray Cattell referred to as a 'Sleeping Beauty', is much older than it looks and is an example of a fourteenth century cruciform church, the north tower being a fifteenth century addition. How-

ever, in an appeal that was launched to preserve it, some years ago, it was stated that it was probable that the foundations and tower are Saxon and that is very old!

The church was originally a daughter church of Yealmpton, fulfilling most roles expected of such a building. How-ever, until the fifteenth century, when-ever one of the Noss Mayo 'flock' died the body had to be taken to Yealmpton for burial. This journey, particularly in depths of winter, would have been a tough one. The Bishop of Exeter was petitioned, the appeal being made with a degree of passion and forcefulness. The parishioners mooted the point that if they were all away, well inland, then enemies of the king could steal in, loot, rob and pillage with nobody to stop them. This and other persuasive remarks won them the right to bury their dead here at the coastal church. After all the sound of the sea was familiar to most of them as many of those laid to rest here were fishermen. Some of the 'residents' of this burial place originally lived on the Wembury side of the Yealm inlet. When it was time for their funerals they were taken on the tide to Bridgend; then their coffins were placed in farm waggons and carried over the hills to their last resting place.

Most of the time this church enjoyed its sheltered position well out of range of the prevailing south westerlies that can cause such havoc in Bigbury Bay. The church was then used once every three weeks for services. However, the sea is a potent force and in 1839 the elements contrived to lash this little church. A fierce south-easterly gale caused extensive damage to the fabric of the church. The locals adapted to the circumstances by holding services in the Chapel of Rest at Noss Mayo. The move, closer to home for most worshippers, was a lasting one. In 1862 this chapel was granted a licence so that weddings could be held, later becoming the village school.

This picture was taken alongside the 'chute', now more commonly called the 'fountain', next to the Chapel of Rest at Noss Mayo. Mr Harrison, headmaster, is on the right in the front row.

Even though the alternative venue in Noss Mayo was used, St Peter's wasn't completely forsaken, for occasional services were held on Sunday afternoons until 1868 when, on Easter morning, yet another terrific storm brought the roof down and effected much structural damage, the only major item to survive being the font.

By now the building had become unsafe but the arrival of Edward Charles Baring was to make a lasting change with the new parish church, also St Peter, on that prominent spot in Noss Mayo. It's believed, by some, that the church at the coast had the words 'the Poor Fisherman' added at this time to help differentiate it from its new successor. However, many also think that it always had this title for it was a place where fishermen worshipped for centuries. In the graveyard many of them are buried with their wives, along with unfortunate shipwreck victims and even a pirate. Renovation work was carried out to the graveyard and this continued to be used. St Peter is the Patron Saint of all fishermen so with such a maritime location the name is perfect for this church. Articles written many years ago suggest that Revelstoke was a small village below the church but that, like Hallsands in Start Bay, it was washed away in times of storm and tempest.

Nature has a way of reclaiming its land from the hand of man. The following years of neglect saw the church become overgrown, like some castle in a fairy story put into a deep sleep. In the 1960s caring local people decided that something really ought to be done to save the ruin. They sought money and help from the 'Redundant Churches Fund' which was forthcoming, enough to effect the major repairs needed to maintain the fabric of the ancient building. The RCF are now responsible for the church but a small management committee still give it a lot of loving attention.

It is recommended that those having gone down to see the ruined church should regain the coast path by returning up the road to the same point where they left it. Here it is stated that it's five miles to Noss Mayo but as walks go it's one of the easier five mile walks in Devon.

The way ahead now skirts the top of Centry Wood before emerging onto Stoke Down. It's important that from now on dogs are kept on leads for the cliffs of this section of coastline are populated with large numbers of grazing sheep. At different vantage points, along this stretch of coast, are a number of stone-built benches, so if you want to rest your loins there are places to sit awhile all enjoying magnificent views. There are also some super spots for picnics. The going is now easy and straightforward as a succession of open downs are passed and the walk, which was a good one, now becomes a great one! The path curves around high above Swale Cove and rises over Netton Down. In Victorian times a flagstaff existed here to warn people that when rifle firing took place there would be no access. Before Netton Down gives way to Snellings Down the OS map shows that two tiny coves, hundreds of feet below, are called Little Bloody Cove and Bloody Cove, a reminder, if one was needed, that this coastline has claimed the lives of many. It was above Bloody Cove that the 500 yard and 600 yard rifle range marker points were placed, the targets being to the east on the side of Stoke Down or Point above Swale Cove.

The almost black coastal rocks are thrust up almost into a right angle and must look daunting to anyone drifting helplessly towards the shore! The carriageway carries us over Snellings Down to reach the remains of the signal station on Gunrow's Down. This was just one of a great number of coastal protection works built along the English Channel coast from about 1794. There was a genuine fear that Napoleon would invade so little was left to chance in an age when communications were primitive by modern standards.

The first sighting of the triangular-shaped Great Mew Stone is gained from this lofty location, whilst hundreds of feet below the path Hilsea Point makes a formidable promontory. Just to the north of it we pass East Hollicombes, one of the two locations where stone was quarried for the building of Noss Mayo's beautiful parish church. The drive now goes gently upwards to a point where a track comes in from the nearby National Trust car park. As far as Warren Cottage the route has a more solid surface as it curves sharply around the top of the hillside.

Warren Cottage was built as the home of the warrener who managed the warren where, within a walled enclosure, rabbits were bred for both their fur and their flesh. Warren Cottage was cleverly constructed to protect it from the prevailing wind. The 'right of way' continues through the curtilage of Warren Cottage but an alternative route deviates to the south of the carriageway for a short distance before rejoining it for another level, straight section across The Warren. Here there is yet another stone bench, this time of granite and engraved '1908 CNE 1980'. Once when I walked this route I was just

thinking how peaceful and serene this spot was, only to be scared out of my wits by several loud booming sounds. These emanated from the gunnery school at HMS *Cambridge* on land opposite the Great Mew Stone!

Soon the carriageway starts to curve around, above Mouthstone Point, from a NNE alignment to a more easterly direction as the mouth of the Yealm is reached. Those walkers who don't mind steep slopes can avail themselves of a route, engineered by the National Trust, which leaves the easier walk of the carriageway to drop down to a much lower level on a walk that includes a visit to Cellars Beach before rejoining the carriageway much farther on. There are good views across the bay towards the maritime frontage of Wembury, where the church of St Werburgh, which has family-tree links with the famous playwright, John Galsworthy, is a dominant landmark.

There is one more opportunity to sit on a bench, this time just before the carriageway descends to enter woods. Below, to the left, is Cellars Beach, a lovely spot on a fine day.

The carriageway continues to drop steadily down and around to the terrace of attractive Coastguard Cottages. Just beyond here and behind a stone wall, on the right of the path is Battery Cottage.

This most desirable property, and twelve acres of land, including a length of the foreshore, were put up for sale, by auction, on Tuesday, 29 September 1929 and advertised as such: "This house, originally part of Membland Hall estate, was built regardless of cost, and is fitted with every possible convenience." All the principal rooms had leaded light windows and Staffordshire grates. It went on to describe the many spacious rooms, the magnificent views and the roomy garage. Outside of this was a covered forecourt for washing vehicles. There was also a chauffeur's room. Cellars Beach was included for good measure. How the 'other half' live! Since then the building has undergone change and those with a fine eye for detail may just notice the galleon-like weather-vane on top of it. The gardens behind it have many subtropical plants, showing the sheltered nature of this site. At the same 1929 auction 'lot 2' was 'Old Cellars' Meadow', an area of almost thirteen acres on land below Battery Cottage. This parcel of land "… occupies one of the most magnificent positions on the South Devon coast, at the entrance to the famous Membland Drives and a situation without parallel as a Building Site for the erection of marine residences."

The woods that line this southern bank of the creek, from Battery Point to Noss, which we now continue through, were also planted by Lord Revelstoke. In older postcard views this hillside appears much more barren, nowhere near as pretty as it is now. However, the views of the estuary are restricted to peeps through the foliage. The rest of the way

to Noss Mayo lies along the road but as it's one long cul-de-sac it does not get a lot of traffic.

The ferry point on this, the Noss side of the estuary, is called Wide Slip. Here a board gives details of ferry times and beside it there is a list of all the traders and places of worship in the twin villages. This, no doubt, was put here to encourage all those hundreds of people who 'do' the South Devon Coastal Path not to miss out, through crossing by ferry from Warren Point to here and immediately proceeding along the coastal path.

Carry on along the road beside the estuary and soon you will need to slow your walking speed down to under thirty miles per hour! Just before the speed restriction signs you will notice a flight of steps leading into the woods. Here a sign tells us that Mrs Doris Spence kindly donated these woods to the National Trust in 1972. The local villagers rallied around to collect a large sum of money to enable these woods to be managed and maintained 'in perpetuity'.

Now we are back in Noss Mayo, a land of pretty cottages, many with appropriate names. The road turns the corner to reach the steps leading to the Voss. However if the tide is in or there is an appreciation of attractive villages it's far better to walk around Noss Creek. It's not a long detour! Those who do so will pass Pink Cottage which is, not surprisingly, pink and another cottage, Blue Shutters, which is also true to its name. At the end of the road there is the Tilly Institute. This building was first built in 1843 and extended some 35 years later as the village school. In Victorian times the teacher used to live on site. It became a Baring property but the enormous estate was sold to Sir William Gray, just before the First World War. In 1920 he sold off the estate in parts. The villagers asked him if they could have the building which he kindly gave to them. He asked them if they would name it in honour of Lt Col Charles Wynn Tilly who was

the last bailiff of the estate. He was killed as the War drew to a close. This listed building is held in trust for the residents and makes an excellent meeting place.

Passing in front of it the road now bears sharply left. Turn left, by Bruar Cottage and stroll along the other side of the Noss Creek past the Methodist Church (1870) where nearby, and on the opposite side of the road, you might spot this delightful message on a garden gate. And you thought it was just the scented aroma of the estuary mud? Continue past Voss Cottage, where Jenie Allen makes her famous marmalade. Here, to this day, the top shelf of the apple-rack has marmalades especially reserved for members of the Baring Family. Then on past the Swan Inn and the Post Office, climb the short but steep hill and continue along the hillside to Junket Corner. Here bear left and before you know it you will have passed many pretty dwellings like Rose Cottage and more converted buildings to get back to the starting point at Bridgend. You have covered at least eight miles, a little more if you went down to see the ruined church. They say the only way to really get to know a place is to walk it and if you have read the text as you have gone along you should know a little more about this wonderful part of Devon.

Newton and Noss now attract a lot of retired, professional people who see the Yealm, and the banks of Newton and Noss Creeks in particular, as the ideal quiet backwater in which to spend their twilight years. As we have seen, they live in the shadow of many who have been here before them. It is rumoured that John Wesley fled from Plymouth in June 1747 only to make haste to

(On the left) the Kitley Belle *at Noss Mayo*

Newton Ferrers, where he sought refuge at a cottage now called 'End of the Strand'. The late Rev. Hugh Grimes, who lived at the Cliffside Hotel, spent his 90th and last year, in 1963, trying to get to the truth of this story. There's no real reason why it shouldn't be true for Wesley was a familiar traveller in Devon, Newton Ferrers being no different from any of the other places where he laid his weary head after a day of preaching. I wonder what Wesley would have made of it had he been still been around to see the Rev. Grimes in his early 'morning glory' whilst enjoying his daily 'skinny-dip' in 'The Pool', something that the vicar must have found revitalising. No wonder the good reverend lived such a long and active life. And what a wonderful place to have lived it, too!

Newton Ferrers and Noss Mayo